My Little Sikh Handbook

ARTIKA AURORA BAKSHI

tara
India Research Press

tara
India Research Press
Flat. 6, Khan Market, New Delhi - 110 003
Ph: 24694610; Fax : 24618637
www.indiaresearchpress.com
contact@indiaresearchpress.com

2018
Reprint 2023

MY LITTLE SIKH HANDBOOK
Artika Aurora Bakshi

Layout and Design Bhavi Mehta

ISBN : 978-81-8386-142-7

Printed and bound in India for Tara-India Research Press

This handbook belongs to

For Hashmat & Himmat

- my joy and my strength!

It was a grey day.

The winter rain made everyone run into the warmth of their homes.

Himmat and Nanki were busy playing Monopoly.

Mummy was sitting by the fireplace reading her book, while Papa was busy watching TV, getting upset with Team India's average performance against Sri Lanka.

"Mummy, I don't want to play with Himmat. He is a sore loser," complained Nanki.

"What do you mean, Nanki Bhenji?" Himmat interrupted.

Mummy knew that both children were tired after a long day staying indoors. She left her book and asked them to come and sit with her.

"Let's forget Monopoly and play another game," she coaxed them.

"Not one of your quiz games," Nanki groaned.

"But I like those games," beamed Himmat.

Mummy got up and brought some paper. She quickly sorted out the sheets and gave them to Himmat and Nanki.

"The first one to finish will get 5 points," she winked.

Himmat and Nanki sprawled on the rug near Mummy and starting working on their activity sheets.

It was a connect the dots and colour activity.

Nanki and Himmat looked excited as they had an idea whose picture it was.

1

ACTIVITY 1:

Connect the dots to see whose picture this is and colour

"Fabulous," clapped Mummy. **"Who remembers the three main teachings of Guru Nanak Dev Ji?"**

Nanki and Himmat looked at each other and beamed. Their school had organised a special assembly a few months back and the children had talked about the teachings of the 10 Sikh gurus. Himmat had also made a poster of **Guru Nanak Dev Ji**, with three bags, with the three tenets of Sikhism written on them.

"Naam Japna ....," said Himmat.

"**Kirat Karna,"** piped up Nanki.

"And, **Vand Chakna,"** both of them said in unison.

"Excellent," Mummy hugged them tightly. "**Vand Chakna** means to share what you have with others. **Kirat Karna** means to always do everything honestly and most importantly, **Naam Japna** tells you to always remember God and say his name with a pure heart."

"Mummy, I recite the **Mool Mantra** everyday while getting ready for school," said Himmat.

"That's really lovely, Himmat. We have so much to be thankful for."

Mummy gave him a kiss. **"Our first guru, Guru Nanak Dev Ji** was born in **1469** at **Talwandi."**

"It's now in Pakistan and the gurdwara is called **Nankana Sahib**," added Nanki. "His sister's name was **Nanki** too just like me!"

"Yes Nanki, we have named you after **Bibi Nanki. Guru Nanak Dev Ji** was very close to his sister. She loved him dearly and always knew that he was special."

Himmat didn't want to feel left out and quickly said, "Guru ji told everyone about ONE God. He travelled all over with his companions **Bala** and **Mardana**."

"Do either of you know who became the guru after **Guru Nanak Dev Ji** passed away?"

Nanki exclaimed, " **Guru Angad Dev Ji!**"

"And then came **Guru Amar Das Ji!**", said Himmat.

"Right! **Guru Amar Das Ji** started the tradition of **langar,**" Mummy smiled. "Now the next activity. Five points again."

ACTIVITY 2:

Connect the dots and colour the Langar (Community Kitchen)

Each gurdwara has a langar where all people are welcome to a free meal.

The basic langar fare consists of daal (lentils), parshada (baked Indian bread), a vegetable and kheer (rice pudding).

All the food is vegetarian so that no religious group is offended.

Everyone eats together irrespective of colour, religion or social status.

Volunteers cook and serve in the langar.

"After **Guru Amar Das Ji**, came **Guru Ram Das Ji**. He founded the city where Nanaji and Naniji live," Nanki said excitedly. She had finished her activity sheet already.

Nanaji had given them a book on the history of **Amritsar.** The children knew that Amritsar got its name from the **Amrit Sarovar** (the holy tank).

Himmat was still struggling with his dots. Nanki went closer and helped him.

"Himmat do you know who became the guru after him?" Mummy asked.

"The fifth guru was **Guru Arjan Dev Ji!** I also know that his mother was **Bibi Bhani**, the daughter of our third guru. She was the wife of **Guru Ram Das Ji**," Himmat beamed.

"**Guru Arjan Dev Ji** also compiled the **Adi Granth,** now known as **Guru Granth Sahib.** It contains the teachings of all the gurus and other famous saints," Mummy told them.

"What next?" Nanki and Himmat asked excitedly.

"The first one to complete the next task gets another five points. I have a very special prize for the final winner," Mummy said.

ੴ

3

ACTIVITY 3:

Connect the dots and colour the Golden Temple, Amritsar

* The Golden Temple also known as Harmandir Sahib is the most important religious center for the Sikhs.
* It has doors in all four directions indicating that it is open to all people.
* It was built by Guru Arjan Dev Ji.
* It is called the Golden Temple because of the gold gilded exterior walls of the temple.
* Harmandir Sahib is also called Darbar Sahib.

When both the children finished the activity, Mummy told them about **Guru Arjan Dev Ji** sacrificing his life for his principles. After his martyrdom, his son, **Guru Hargobind Ji** became the sixth guru. He carried two swords, representing military strength, **"miri"** and spiritual power, **"piri"**. He was the first Sikh guru to raise an army against Mughal injustice.

"When Emperor Jahangir arrested him, he continued to stand for what he believed in. Upon his release from prison, he demanded the release of 52 kings, who were also imprisoned. That day is celebrated as **Bandi Chorh Diwas,** which falls a few days before Diwali. The guru returned to Amritsar on Diwali day," she said.

By this time, Papa had also left the cricket match and joined them.

"And then came **Guru Har Rai Ji,** who was the grandson of **Guru Hargobind Ji**. He preached daily **simran** and respect for ***Gurbani* (Words of Gurus),"** Papa said. "Where is the chart that I printed out for you? Do you colour the star for everyday that you do **simran**?"

4

ACTIVITY 4:

Colour a star for every day of simran

ੴ

ਸਤਿ ਨਾਮੁ ਕਰਤਾ ਪੁਰਖੁ ਨਿਰਭਉ ਨਿਰਵੈਰੁ ਅਕਾਲ ਮੂਰਤਿ ਅਜੂਨੀ ਸੈਭੰ ਗੁਰ ਪ੍ਰਸਾਦਿ ||

|| ਜਪੁ ||

Ik onkar sat nam karta purakh nir bhau nir vair

akal murat ajuni saibhang gur prasaad ||

|| jap ||

"Then came **Guru Har Krishan Ji.** He was only five when he became the guru. He died three years later in Delhi. **Gurdwara Bangla Sahib** stands where he stayed, while in Delhi. His last words were, ***"Baba Bakale",*** which pointed the Sikhs to their ninth guru, **Guru Tegh Bahadur Ji**. Guru ji was the youngest son of **Guru Hargobind Ji** and was staying in Bakala," Papa explained.

"I know that **Guru Tegh Bahadur Ji** was beheaded by Emperor Aurangzeb at **Gurdwara Sisganj,"** said Himmat. "Mummy had taken us there. Guru ji did not let Aurangzeb convert people forcefully to Islam. After him, his son, our tenth guru, **Guru Gobind Singh Ji** fought against the Mughals."

"Very good, Himmat! And now, the next activity."

5 ACTIVITY 5:

Colour the image of Guru Gobind Singh Ji

In **1699**, Guru Gobind Singh Ji chose Vaisakhi as the occasion to transform the Sikhs into a family of soldier saints, known as the *Khalsa Panth*.

The *Khalsa* was founded in Anandpur Sahib.

During the Vaisakhi festival, Guru Gobind Singh Ji came out of a tent carrying a sword. He challenged the gathering for anyone who was prepared to give his life to come into the tent. One brave gentleman volunteered and went into the tent with him. The Guru returned alone with his sword covered in blood. He then requested another volunteer and repeated the same action until five men disappeared into the tent. The crowd was very concerned until they saw five men return wearing turbans with the Guru.

These five men became known as the *Panj Piare*, or the Beloved Five.

"Do you know that Anandpur Sahib is also famous for Hola Mohalla?" added Papa. "Sikhs from all over gather there every year for a fair. There is music, poetry, langar and martial arts display. You can see little children practicing gatka and riding horses daringly."

"What's gatka?" asked Himmat.

"It is an old form of martial arts using swords, sticks, clubs and wheels," explained Papa.

"And it's really colourful!!!!" beamed Nanki. "I saw it on TV. Can we please go there one time?"

"Do you know that Sikhism is one of the world's youngest religions, being founded just over 500 years ago?" Papa asked.

"The word '**Sikh**' means 'disciple' and Sikhs are disciples of 'ONE' God and they follow the writings and teachings of the ten Sikh gurus," Mummy added.

"You told us about the **Guru Granth Sahib**," Himmat added proudly. Nanki further told Himmat what she had learnt in her religious studies class.

"Sikhism teaches that there is only 'ONE' God. All men and women are equal. The way to reach God is by remembering his name always. Sikhs should work hard and live honestly. Sharing and community service are essential duties of all Sikhs," she said proudly."Always remember that Sikhism teaches you to
respect all religions. Never make fun of your friends' beliefs. The Granth Sahib has the teachings of our gurus, many Hindu and Sufi saints too."

Mummy added strongly. "Even the first stone of Harmandir Sahib in Amritsar was laid by a Sufi saint called **Mian Mir**."

"Let's get on with the next activity now. Five more points," winked Papa.

ACTIVITY 6:

Match the following:-

Time.........................

Talwandi	The 2nd guru of the Sikhs
Guru Angad Dev Ji	The swords of soldier and saint worn by Guru Hargobind Ji
Guru ka Langar	The place where Guru Har Krishan Ji stayed, when he visited Delhi
Amritsar	The city founded by Guru Ram Das Ji
Guru Arjan Dev Ji	The gurdwara in Chandni Chowk, Delhi, where Guru Tegh Bahadar Ji was beheaded
Miri Piri	Started by the 10th guru, Guru Gobind Singh Ji
Guru Har Rai Ji	The 7th guru of the Sikhs
Gurdwara Bangla Sahib	Compiled the Guru Granth Sahib
Sis Ganj Sahib	The birthplace of Guru Nanak Dev Ji, the 1st guru of the Sikhs
Khalsa Panth	Was started by Guru Amar Das Ji

7

ACTIVITY 7:

Word Search: Find the five Ks of Sikhism:

A	K	A	N	G	A
B	A	E	K	F	A
K	C	F	A	G	K
I	C	G	B	H	A
R	H	H	C	I	R
P	A	I	D	J	A
A	C	J	E	K	B
N	D	K	E	S	H

Time.....................

The five Ks are:

KIRPAN (dagger) - The kirpan symbolises the Sikhs' strong sense of responsibility and protection of the weak.

KANGA (comb) - A kanga is a small comb, neatly tucked in a Sikh's hair to keep it clean and untangled.

KARA (metal bracelet) - A kara is round and worn on the right wrist to remind Sikhs of God, who has no beginning and no end.

KESH (hair) - Sikhs are easily recognizable by uncut hair tied up in their turbans or head scarves.

KACCHA (undershorts) - The kaccha reminds the Sikhs to always follow restrain and modesty.

"Five more points up for grabs," Mummy said. "For this activity, Papa can help Nanki and I will be in Himmat's team."

"Yipeeeeee!!!!!".

Mummy gave both a sheet of paper with an outline of a **"KHANDA."**

THE KHANDA -
a double edged sword that symbolises belief in the 'ONE' God

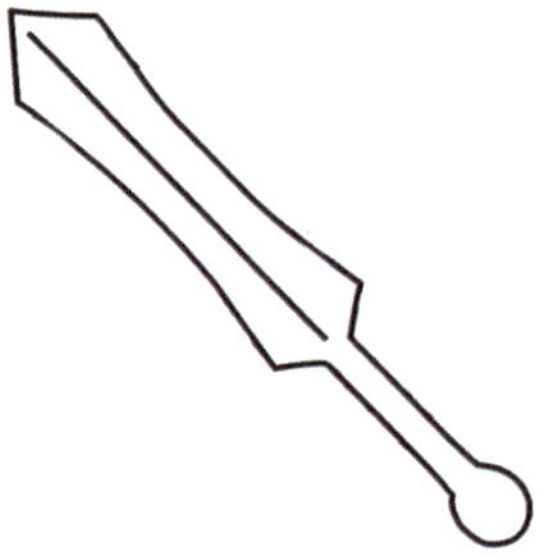

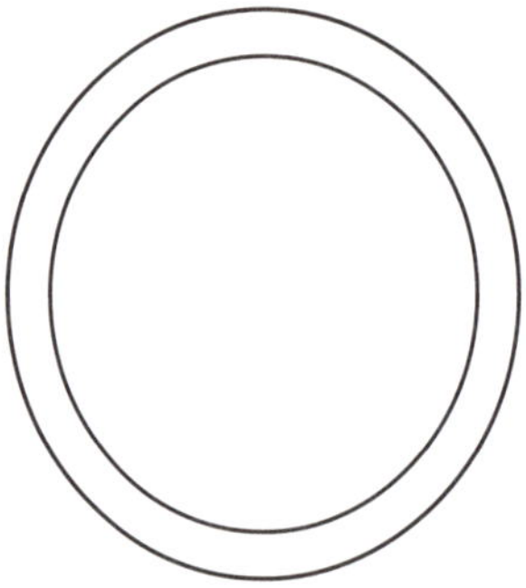

THE CHAKKAR -
a disc that symbolises the 'ONE' God without any beginning or end

THE TWO CROSSED KIRPANS -
symbolising spirituality and physical strength

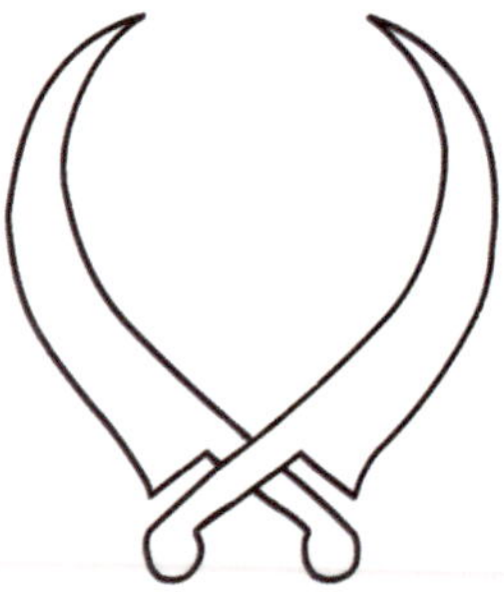

ACTIVITY 8:

8 Colour the Khanda and try to draw it yourself!

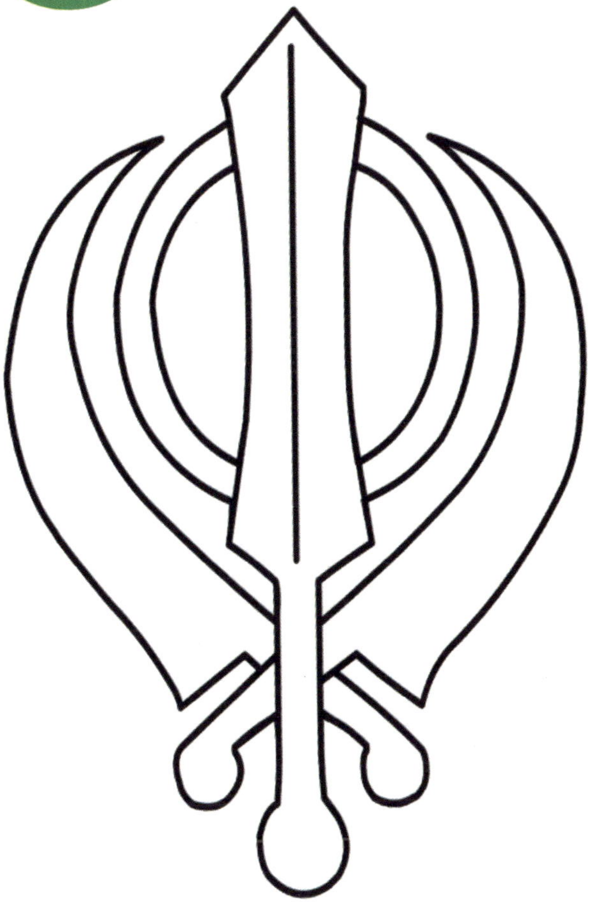

Now draw here:

"And now, the next activity," Mummy said.

"Mummy, what's the prize?" Himmat could not wait any longer. He knew that he was behind Nanki by just five points. Both had completed all the activities so far at almost the same time. He had only lost out to his bhenji in one colouring activity because his colour pencils has needed to be sharpened.

"It's a surprise, Himmat. Let's get on to the next set," Mummy smiled.

Himmat could not hide his excitement. His eyes shone brightly as he got ready for the next activity.

9

ACTIVITY 9:

Acrostic Poem Nishan Sahib

The Nishan Sahib is the Sikh flag that flies high outside every gurdwara. The Nishan Sahib is saffron in colour with a khanda on top of the flag post.

Draw the Nishan Sahib and colour it saffron.

N

I

Super

H

A

Nice

S

A

H

I

Blessed

10 Word Search:

ACTIVITY 10:

Time..........................

GIDDA, SINGH, GURDWARA, AMRIT, SIKH, KAUR, LANGAR, SEWA, BHANGRA, KARAH PARSHAD

A	B	C	D	E	F	G	A	S	I	N	G	H
F	E	D	C	B	A	G	F	E	D	C	B	A
G	I	D	D	A	A	B	C	D	E	F	K	G
A	U	A	B	C	D	E	F	G	A	B	A	F
B	A	R	B	C	D	E	F	G	A	B	R	E
C	A	B	D	C	D	E	F	G	B	A	A	D
D	A	B	C	W	D	E	F	G	H	B	H	C
E	A	B	C	D	A	E	F	G	A	C	P	B
F	A	B	C	M	D	R	E	F	N	D	A	A
G	S	A	R	A	B	L	A	N	G	A	R	G
A	G	I	F	E	D	C	B	A	R	E	S	F
B	T	A	K	B	C	S	E	W	A	F	H	E
C	A	B	A	H	A	B	C	D	E	G	A	D
D	B	A	U	G	F	E	D	C	B	A	D	C
E	F	G	R	A	B	C	D	E	F	G	A	B

DID YOU KNOW?

GIDDA - folk dance of women in Punjab

SINGH - every Sikh male uses this as part of his name; Singh means 'lion'

GURDWARA - Sikh temple of worship

AMRIT - nectar or holy water

SIKH - follower of Sikhism; Sikh means 'to learn'

KAUR - every Sikh female uses this as part of her name; Kaur means 'princess'

LANGAR - community food kitchen

SEWA - selfless service; a must for all Sikhs

BHANGRA - folk dance of men in Punjab

KARAH PARSHAD - blessed halwa sweet pudding made out of wheat flour and sugar

With all the activities done, it was time for Mummy to give the much-awaited prize.

"Both of you did equally well and both of you will get a prize each," Mummy gave them a tight hug each.

"But Mummy, I finished before Himmat!" protested Nanki.

Himmat did the bhangra in delight and both Papa and Mummy laughed. Nanki seemed to be sulking. Mummy went to her room and came back with two books.

"When I was your age, my mother gave me a book just like the one I have brought for you," Mummy smiled, remembering her mother.

"This book is called My Little Sikh Handbook. You will love the activities in it. There are blank pages in this too, where you can write your special dreams and thoughts," Mummy said opening the book to show Nanki and Himmat.

Himmat and Nanki jumped with joy and gave Mummy a big hug. They jumped onto Papa's lap to show him their prizes.

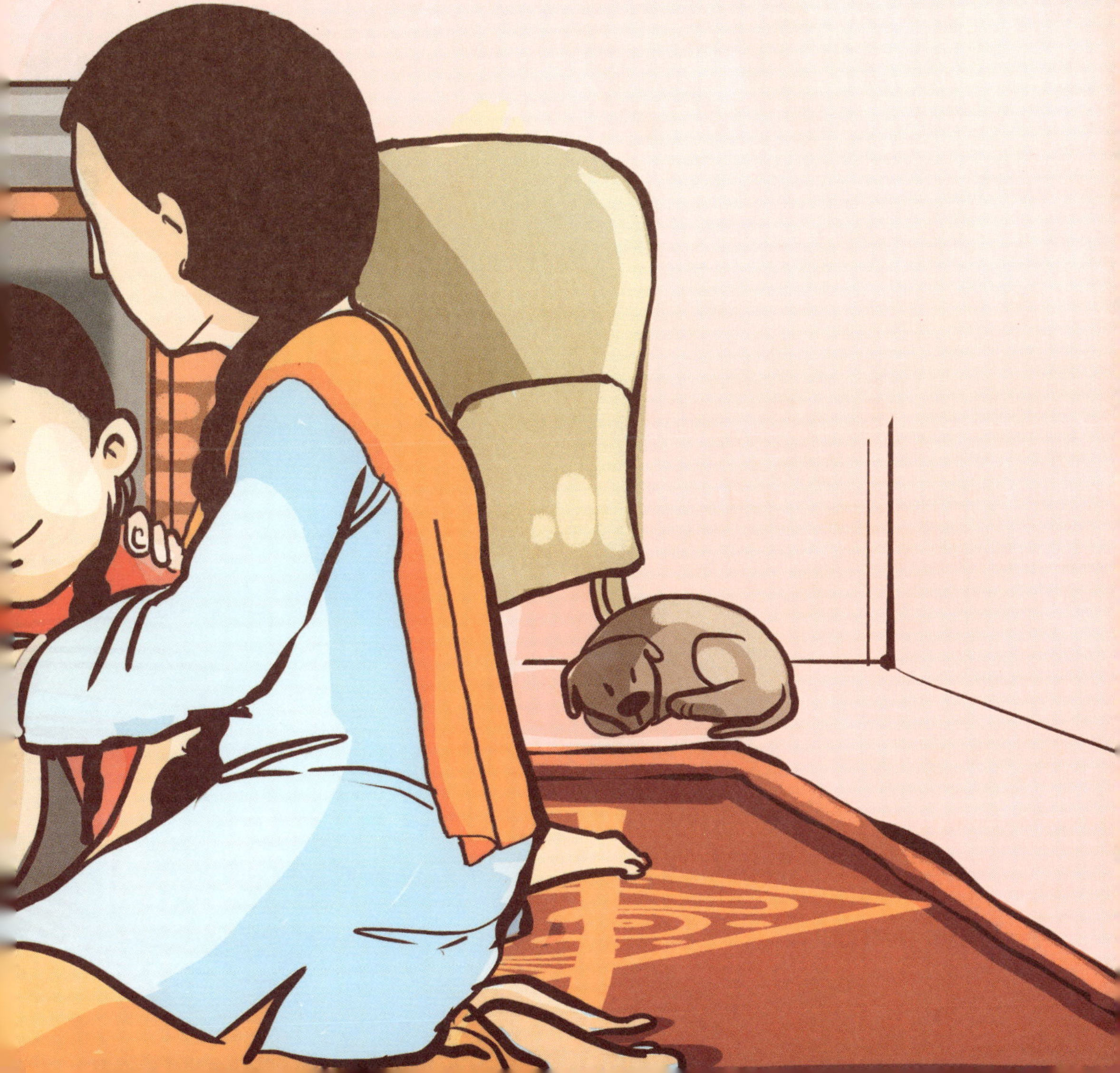

MY PAGES OF SIKH HISTORY

The Gurmukhi Alphabet

ੳ	ਅ	ੲ	ਸ	ਹ	ਕ	ਖ	ਗ
OORHAA	AIRHAA	EERHEE	SASSAA	HAHA	KAKKAA	KHAKHKHAA	GAGGAA
ਘ	ਙ	ਚ	ਛ	ਜ	ਝ	ਞ	ਟ
GHAGGAA	NGANNGAA	CHACHCHAA	CHHACHH	JAJJAA	JHAJJAA	NJANNJAA	TAINKAA
ਠ	ਡ	ਢ	ਣ	ਤ	ਥ	ਦ	ਧ
THATHTHAA	DADDAA	DHADDAA	NHAANHAA	TATTAA	THATHTHAA	DADDAA	DHADDAA
ਨ	ਪ	ਫ	ਬ	ਭ	ਮ	ਯ	ਰ
NANNAA	PAPPAA	PHAPHPHAA	BABBAA	BHABBAA	MAMMAA	YAYYAA	RAARAA
ਲ	ਵ	ੜ	ਸ਼	ਖ਼	ਗ਼	ਜ਼	ਫ਼
LALLAA	VAVVAA	RHAARHAA	SHASHA	KHHAKHH	GHAGGHAA	ZAZZAA	FAFFAA
ਲ਼	#ਾ	ਿ#	#ੀ	#ੁ	#ੂ	#ੇ	#ੈ
LALLAA	CAR	KICK	DEEP	LOOK	SOUP	LATE	GLAD
#ੋ	#ੌ						
GO	CROWN						

੧	੨	੩	੪	੫	੬	੭	੮
1	2	3	4	5	6	7	8
੯	੦						
9	0						

The Gurmukhi Alphabet Write and Learn

ੳ ਅ ੲ ਸ ਹ ਕ

ਖ ਗ ਘ ਙ ਚ ਛ

ਜ ਝ ਞ ਟ ਠ ਡ

The Gurmukhi Alphabet Write and Learn

ਢ ਣ ਤ ਥ ਦ ਧ

ਨ ਪ ਫ ਬ ਭ ਮ

ਯ ਰ ਲ ਵ ੜ ਸ਼

The Gurmukhi Alphabet Write and Learn

ਖ਼ ਗ਼ ਜ਼ ਫ਼ ਲ਼ ੴ

੧ ੨ ੩ ੪ ੫

੬ ੭ ੮ ੯ ੦

ACKNOWLEDGEMENTS

This book is my passionate offering to all Sikh families. The value system in my home is very strong and for my husband and I, bringing up our boys in the right way has been of prime importance. Through colouring activities, reading sessions and endless discussions (which were always very exciting) this journey has been a memorable one.

The story of Himmat and Nanki is a glimpse into our life as a family, when the boys were growing up.

I would like to thank my first readers for their encouragement. Maninder, Hashmat, Himmat, Karen and Preeti, couldn't have done it without your feedback.

To Anuj Bahri, thank you for helping me bring this book to where it is today. I was meant to work with you on this.

Priyankar Gupta, your illustrations make the story come alive. Bhavi Mehta, for your designing skills. A special thank you to www.connectthedots101.com and www.sikhnet.com for letting me use some of their activities.

ABOUT THE AUTHOR

An avid reader, a teacher, a book critique, an aspiring writer, but most importantly a mother, Artika Aurora Bakshi lives in a world of words. This is her first children's book. Artika's first story was published on www.storymirror.com. She is currently working on her next children's book and a series of other short stories.